Chicago Tribune

John Paul II

THE EPIC LIFE OF A PILGRIM POPE

TRIUMPH
BOOKS
CHICAGO

The CD-ROM "Be not afraid: The epic papacy of John Paul II" brings to life one of the towering figures of our times through original **multimedia storytelling**. In nine **interactive tales**, readers experience history unfolding through text; more than 350 photographs; exclusive **video interviews** with former U.S. President George H.W. Bush, former Polish President Lech Walesa and other newsmakers; nearly **100 mini-biographies**; archival footage; papal writings and addresses; and more than **200 Chicago Tribune articles**.

To experience the CD-ROM, users will need:
A PC with a Pentium III processor or better, 128MB of RAM (256 preferred), Windows 2000 or Windows XP operating system, a 4x or faster CD-ROM drive, a minimum screen resolution of 800x600, Flash and QuickTime software (available on the CD-ROM)
or
A Macintosh with 500MHz processor or better (G4 or G5), 128MB of RAM (256 preferred), OS 9 or OS X operating system, a 4x or faster CD-ROM drive, a minimum screen resolution of 800x600, Flash and QuickTime software (available free on the Internet)

Library of Congress Control Number: 2005901721

This book is available in quantity at special discounts for your group or organization. For further information, contact:

Triumph Books
601 South LaSalle Street
Suite 500
Chicago, Illinois 60605
(312) 939-3330
Fax (312) 663-3557

Printed in U.S.A.
ISBN-13: 978-1-57243-704-3
ISBN-10: 1-57243-704-9
Design by Eileen Wagner, Wagner/Donovan, Chicago, Illinois

Pope John Paul II, the most traveled pontiff in history, was greeted by enthusiastic multitudes—hundreds of thousands, even millions of people—in country after country over more than a quarter century. Some say he was seen in person by more people than anyone who ever lived.

Each of his journeys had a purpose. In some places, he emphasized the traditional stands of the church on issues such as abortion, women in the clergy and the evils of materialism. Some would say bravely while others would say stubbornly, he presented those positions to the very audiences who least wanted to hear them. He traveled to confront communism that ruled his native Poland—and, through his visits, helped end its grip. He spoke out against unbridled capitalism, dehumanizing globalism and rampant consumerism.

His long global odyssey seemed, in a way, a series of family visits, calling on the world's 1 billion Roman Catholics. In historic journeys to mend centuries-old estrangements, he also reached out to members of other faiths.

The photos documenting his travels include strikingly similar images: huge crowds of people reaching out to touch him, a reaction perhaps to having been so deeply touched by him. Though the faces change across racial and ethnic boundaries—Polish-Americans in Chicago, colorfully dressed Nigerians, young girls in Portugal, Cubans gathered in Havana's Revolution Plaza—their expressions of faith and hope remain remarkably the same.

The family he touched was humanity. ◼

Czestochowa, Poland, 1979

The holy shrine at
Fatima, Portugal, 2000

Airport at Yaoundé, capital of Cameroon, 1995

Arriving at the Canadian capital, Ottawa,
via the Rideau Canal, 1984

As was his custom, kissing the ground upon
landing, here at Auckland, New Zealand, 1986

CONTENTS

Maribor, Slovenia, 1999

Called to a lead role on the world stage

Double rows of giant stone colonnades curve out on either side of St. Peter's Square, ready to sweep hundreds of thousands of people into a magnificent architectural embrace. The basilica—its enormous archways, its towering columns and outsize statues, all forced into perspective by the great expanse of the facade and dome—seems to exert its own gravity, pulling crowds into the center of Roman Catholicism.

Even when people crowd into the square, covering every last cobblestone, they do not dominate it. From a distance the effect is that of an animated carpet, changing the texture of the plaza without intruding upon its higher drama. The scale of the place is not about individuals.

Yet on Oct. 22, 1978, a man of average height and middle age, a foreigner with little public profile, commanded that plaza in a way few of his predecessors ever had.

Pope John Paul II had been the surprise choice of the Catholic Church's cardinals just days earlier. For the first time in four centuries, a non-Italian had been picked as the bishop of Rome. Outside church circles, few in the West knew much about the Polish churchman who had appeared on the balcony of St. Peter's that night, announced for the first time to the perplexed crowd below.

Now he was back in the square, looking robust in his white and gold finery, looking at home in the baroque grandeur of the setting, looking equal to a job that had seemed to swallow so many of his predecessors.

When the cardinals came forward, one by one, to pay their respects to the new pope, he prevented many of them from kneeling before him—instead, he grabbed them in a fraternal embrace. After his Polish mentor, Cardinal Stefan Wyszynski, genuflected and kissed John Paul's ring, the pope caught Wyszynski's hand and returned the gesture of affection and honor.

More than 200,000 looked on, including kings and queens, presidents and princes. Millions more watched and listened in what the Vatican said was its largest broadcast audience to that date.

The ritual was ancient and familiar, but the crowds were riveted by the man who infused it with new vigor, radiating good spirits and speaking with passion and a practiced sense of timing—in 11 languages.

"Be not afraid!" he called out in his homily, a baritone refrain that would reverberate through more than 100 trips abroad, in each of his 14 encyclicals and more than 60 other major papal documents.

Newly named pontiff, Oct. 16, 1978

"Be not afraid!"—part command, part prayer—became the driving force of his 26-year papacy, an epic reign that both energized and polarized the Roman Catholic Church.

He came to that inaugural mass a man who had been shaped directly by the great events of his century. He had been born in a brief window of European peace, fired in the kiln of World War II and remained unbowed by decades of communist oppression.

And from that moment in the square, he embarked on a career that would change the course of the world, fueled by faith and sheer dint of will.

Some in his own church complained that John Paul II was a throwback to an earlier kind of pope, imperial and autocratic, bent on quashing dissent. Others said he was ahead of his time, traversing the world many times over to spread his message, the first jet-set pope.

Occasionally prevailing, never surrendering, he proved that the pope needs no military divisions, that spiritual power is a force to be reckoned with even in the midst of secular modernism.

He stared down dictators and clamped down on critics. He was credited with helping to topple the totalitarian government of his native Poland in 1989, leading to the fall of communist Eastern Europe and the Soviet Union.

He was blamed for alienating women and liberal Catholics in the West with rigid stances against women in the priesthood, abortion, birth control and homosexuality. Church insiders chafed against the growing power of the Vatican during his pontificate, and a narrowing of debate.

To the world, he preached hard lessons on money and the me-first destructiveness of individuals and nations. He never hesitated to say what an audience least wanted to hear, yet his unblinking message always carried seeds of hope and love, especially for those who suffer.

He made new efforts to reach out to Orthodox Christians, Jews and Muslims, and he went out of his way to forgive the man who shot and almost killed him in 1981. He encountered virtually every major world leader of the last quarter century, and few were unchanged by the experience.

Fulfilling the prophecy of a close friend, John Paul II led his church into the third millennium of Christianity. Despite the ravages of Parkinson's disease and the lingering effects of an assassination attempt, the pontiff with the iron constitution and steel will celebrated the Jubilee year 2000 that he had so long anticipated. He crowned the momentous event with a historic trip to the Holy Land in March that year, a return to the wellspring of his faith with the world in tow.

His ill health did take a toll on his work. Insiders say that in his last years, the pope focused only on those tasks he felt central to spreading the gospel, while delegating the governance of the church to aides. That withdrawal led to confusion on some doctrinal issues, and left the pope a virtual bystander during the clergy sexual abuse crisis faced by the Catholic Church in the United States.

But for most of his pontificate, John Paul II embodied the power and tradition of Catholicism at a time when the institutions and influence of the church were in flux. Some of his best work carried the essence of the church's titans—the searing clarity of Aquinas, the mysticism of St. John of the Cross—freshening their ancient messages for 1 billion Catholics from Africa to India to Latin America.

Yet he never let his followers forget that he was human. As scandalized aides looked on, the muscular, mountain-climbing pope of the early years would sometimes clown around, pantomiming that he was watching a crowd through binoculars, or donning a sombrero in Mexico.

The bent figure of the final years showed his humanity in other ways. Though unable to hide his pain, he somehow found the energy to walk down the stairs of yet one more airplane, to raise his cane to the cheering crowds that greeted him at every stop. One cardinal marveled at the pope's willingness to display his infirmities to the world, preferring that the world see a pontiff who might drool or lose his voice midsentence rather than a pope who withdrew to the privacy of his Vatican palace.

His secular biographers, who have filled bookshelves with their thick volumes, have agreed on at least this point: John Paul II was one of the most remarkable figures of the last century. Several years ago, his most enthusiastic admirers began calling him "John Paul the Great," a title given officially to only two of the previous 263 popes. Talk of sainthood may not be far behind.

Above: With his mother, Emilia
Right: His father, Karol

The pope did not bother much with such attention. He seldom spoke about himself, except as the visible head of the church.

Yet in the opening lines of "Crossing the Threshold of Hope," the 1994 book-length interview that became perhaps the first international best seller penned by a pope, he paused to note his own sinfulness, his feeling of unworthiness of God's love.

"Every man has learned it. Every successor to Peter has learned it. I learned it very well," he said. "Of what should we not be afraid? We should not fear the truth about ourselves."

Mother's dream for son comes true

Karol Józef Wojtyla was born May 18, 1920, in the small agricultural town of Wadowice, Poland. Though his house was across the street from Wadowice's largest Catholic church, it must have seemed as far from the gilded halls of the Vatican as it was from the moon.

His father, a lieutenant and clerk in the Polish army, was 40; his mother was 36. His only brother was 13. A sister died in infancy before he was born.

They were devout Catholics, especially his mother, who wanted young "Lolek," as she called Karol, to become a priest someday.

But his mother was sickly from the time he was born, and she slowly withdrew from the family's life. She died when Karol was 8, an event that many observers felt shaped his life and ultimately his papacy. His stoic and mystical approach to human suffering may have been formed in that experience, and some believe his tireless devotion to the Virgin Mary had roots there as well.

Karol's older brother, a physician whom he greatly admired, died just three years later, and his father was dead when Karol was 20.

By then, death was all around him. The Nazis had invaded Poland in 1939, and as time went on, they deported many of his Jewish childhood friends, his university professors and anybody

As a bishop, at the
Parthenon, Athens, 1963

In a Polish military training camp, Eastern Poland, 1939
Above: Second from right
Left: Shirtless with friends

who resisted the occupation to concentration camps, including nearby Auschwitz.

Wojtyla himself did forced labor for the Nazis in a quarry and later a chemical factory. At one point during the war, he was struck by a German army truck, an event that was never clearly determined to be accidental or intentional.

Amid that horror, Wojtyla found a secret life, as an actor in an underground theater group, and in a budding spiritual and religious calling that drew him to illegal prayer meetings. Both vocations tugged at him.

In 1942, he surprised his friends by saying that the choice had been made for him: He would be a priest.

Still working at the factory, he began to undertake secret seminary studies. It was a time when Wojtyla broke the tedium of manual labor with his own solitary pursuits. He made his first serious foray into theological reading and developed a prayer life that included hours on his knees or prostrate on a cold floor—a practice he maintained steadfastly for decades to come, beginning each day of his papacy facedown on the floor for hours in solitary prayer.

In 1944, the tide of war was turning against the Nazis, who constantly feared internal uprisings. After a Nazi sweep of Krakow sent thousands of able-bodied Poles to the concentration camps without warning, Archbishop Adam Sapieha, Wojtyla's mentor, took all his secret seminarians into his own mansion, where they hid until the end of the war.

Wojtyla had tried once before to enter the contemplative life of the Carmelite religious order, and as his seminary studies came to a close, he again pressed Sapieha for the chance to cloister himself in a life of prayer and study.

The archbishop would have none of it; on Nov. 1, 1946, he ordained Wojtyla a priest of the Archdiocese of Krakow.

The young priest spent the next two years in Rome, earning a doctorate in theology before he returned to Poland to work as a pastor. He began in a small farming parish, and then moved to a university parish, where his love and talent for working with young people became legend.

He also continued studying, eventually becoming a professor of theology and ethics.

As a priest, on an outing with a Catholic youth group

Pope Pius XII made Wojtyla an auxiliary bishop of Krakow in 1958, three months before he died. When Krakow's archbishop died in 1962, Wojtyla became the temporary head of the archdiocese, just in time to get a seat at the pivotal event of 20th Century Catholicism, the Second Vatican Council. In time, he became the spokesman for the 10 Polish bishops at the council.

Wojtyla, however, was not particularly appreciated by Poland's Cardinal Stefan Wyszynski, a hard-nosed prelate who managed to keep the Polish church alive under communism but often confronted the government.

One of the tacit agreements Wyszynski had made with the secular rulers was that, working from a list approved by the pope, the cardinal would choose three names to fill any vacant bishop's seat in Poland, and forward those to the government. The government could then choose one of those as the new bishop.

But when it came time to appoint a new archbishop of Krakow, government officials had grown weary of Wyszynski and wary of his power. They wanted to appoint an archbishop who would undermine the cardinal, one who would be less political and easier to manipulate.

They ignored Wyszynski's first and second lists of candidates and looked at the politically detached intellectual serving temporarily as bishop of Krakow—Wojtyla—and chose him.

Wyszynski was furious, and initially wouldn't agree. But eventually, when a delegation of priests came forward to support Wojtyla, he gave in, and Wojtyla was appointed archbishop of Krakow in January 1964. The young archbishop—who quickly gained the attention of Pope Paul VI with writings after Vatican II and work on the pope's special commission on birth control—was elevated to cardinal in 1967.

Newly selected cardinal,
Krakow, Poland, 1967

Few predicted election as pope

Even with that quick rise to power, and the clear leadership he began to exert in Poland in the 1970s, few people have ever been brave enough to claim that they believed Wojtyla would become pope.

The conclave that elected Pope John Paul I in 1978 took just four ballots to find a man who satisfied the cardinals, a man seen as more pastoral than ideological. But his death, after just one month in the Vatican, left the cardinals in a much more difficult position.

It was a given that the next pope would be Italian—it had been more than 400 years since a non-Italian had been made the bishop of Rome—but there was a sharp split between two Italian factions. One wanted more reform along the lines of Vatican II, while a more conservative group wanted to consolidate the authority of the pope and of the Vatican staff.

As the cardinals began to search for a way around that disagreement, widening the net to include dozens of candidates from outside Italy, one name began to be mentioned more and more frequently: Cardinal Wojtyla. He was a relative unknown and very young at 58, but a man who had shown himself capable both at the Vatican and in his diocese; a man who was formed by Vatican II, but was not likely to push its church reforms too much further. At a time when the church in the West was divided and dispirited, Wojtyla had brought vigor and growth to a church under communist repression.

On Oct. 16, 1978, the College of Cardinals chose Wojtyla to be the next pope, and he, in turn, chose the name John Paul II, in homage to his three immediate predecessors.

Showing himself to the mystified Italians gathered in St. Peter's Square—who was Wojtyla?—he told them they should correct him if he made mistakes in their language, now his language as well.

John Paul II quickly became known as one of the most approachable popes in history. Soon after he became pope, he officiated at a marriage ceremony for two "commoners," simply because they had asked him.

He made Vatican history on Good Friday in 1980 by putting on a regular priest's vestments, entering a confessional in St. Peter's Basilica and hearing worshipers' confessions for more than an

Greeting pilgrims in St. Peter's Square, Vatican City, 1984

hour and a half. It was a practice that he undertook clandestinely from time to time throughout his papacy. Penitents at St. Peter's soon came to understand that there was always a chance, however small, that the man on the other side of the confessional screen would be the pope.

He loved the crowds that surrounded him on every occasion. He talked and laughed, hugged and blessed people, shook hands. He preferred riding in open vehicles, standing up so people could see him easily.

In one of his first public appearances as pope, the Swiss Guards charged with protecting the pope formed a shoulder-to-shoulder cordon around him to keep the crowd from pressing too close. The pope pushed the guards away, one later recalled, saying, "I don't want gorillas around. I know how to defend myself."

His security team's worst fears materialized on May 13, 1981, when a convicted murderer from Turkey, already on the run, lunged out of the crowd that had gathered in St. Peter's Square for the pope's weekly general audience.

The open popemobile was slowly rolling through the crowd, and Mehmet Ali Agca took two clear shots at the pope. One bullet grazed him; the other wounded him gravely.

As the pope fought for his life in a nearby hospital, it quickly became apparent what deep feelings for him had grown around the world during his 2½ years as bishop of Rome. Even Soviet President Leonid Brezhnev, privately chafing at the loyalty the pope inspired in his Polish homeland, and famed American atheist Madalyn Murray O'Hair expressed their indignation at the assassination attempt and their profound respect for the pope.

For years, investigators tried to find out whether Agca was part of a larger conspiracy against the pope, perhaps one inspired by Eastern European communists who feared the effect of John Paul II's calls for freedom and human dignity. No link was ever proved.

The pope focused his attention instead on learning from his suffering, and forgiving his attacker. On Dec. 27, 1983, the pope visited Agca in a Roman prison for 20 minutes. At the end, the pope once again offered the gunman his forgiveness, and Agca dropped to his knees, kissing the pope's hand.

Seventeen years later, the Vatican's support for clemency for Agca helped earn the gunman's early release from Italian prison and his return to Turkey.

Tireless appetite for world travel

Even more than his personal style, the aspect of John Paul II's papacy that stood out most clearly from his predecessors' was his visibility around the world.

He made more than 100 trips outside Italy, more than 150 within Italy, and personally visited more than 300 of Rome's 334 parishes.

Even allowing for jet airplanes and other technological improvements that made travel much easier for a pope by the late 20th Century, that grueling itinerary dwarfed the efforts of previous popes to get out among the people.

One of his first trips abroad, in the autumn of 1979, brought the pope to Chicago. He was the first pope to visit Chicago, but it was his third trip to the city, where he had courted the huge and loyal Polish population on previous visits as bishop and archbishop. They turned out in droves for his papal visit, lining Milwaukee Avenue and cheering wildly.

To the rest of Chicago's Catholic population, and indeed most of the world, the new pope was something of a mystery. But Chicagoans turned out in force, filling the vast lawn of Grant Park with hundreds of thousands of worshipers for the papal mass.

The pope traced his tireless appetite for travel to an experience he had on his first trip abroad as pontiff, a visit to Mexico in 1979. He was stunned by the millions of people who lined his route, waiting days for a glimpse of the pope.

One of his first stops was the Basilica of Our Lady of Guadalupe, where he spent more than an hour alone, praying before the dark-skinned image of the Virgin Mary that is said to have had a profound impact in the conversion of the indigenous population in Latin America during the 16th and 17th Centuries, eventually creating the largest concentration of Roman Catholics in the world.

It was while praying to the Virgin of Guadalupe, the pope later said, that he had an epiphany, suddenly understanding that it was his mission to become the pilgrim pope, bringing the word of God to people around the world.

Jubilant return to his homeland

Newly determined to spread the gospel in person, the pope decided to visit his homeland, Poland. Though Poland had been for centuries one of Europe's most devoutly Catholic countries, no pope had ever been there. Nor had any pope ever traveled to a communist country. But John Paul II would not rest until he did.

In June 1979, the pope arrived in Poland for what would turn out to be nine days of jubilation unlike anything the nation had ever known.

The homecoming of the beloved churchman, the first Polish pope, carried strong undercurrents of pre-communist patriotism and genuine workers' movements that would challenge the ideology of the government.

But the pope was not looking for a showdown. His focus was on a reawakening of the country's slumbering faith. He prayed at Auschwitz, worshiped at the national shrine of the Black Madonna of Czestochowa, and everywhere invoked the martyr and patron saint of Poland, St. Stanislaw.

More than a million people came to see him in Krakow. It was a turning point in Polish history, one recognized not only in the throngs, but in a disturbed Kremlin as well.

The fire ignited during that visit flared up here and there in the months that followed, most notably in the shipyard labor strikes that were led by workers carrying posters of the pope. From Rome, the pope supported the strikes, sending public and private messages.

The Polish government was in a bind. On one hand, it did not want the pope stirring up further trouble. On the other, it did not feel that it could deny him another visit to Poland without provoking the citizenry to rebellion.

So when the pope returned to his homeland in 1983, both the communists and the pope knew that it would be more than a simple, pastoral visit.

The late Auxiliary Bishop Alfred Abramowicz of Chicago, who spearheaded efforts among Polish Catholics in the United States to aid the church in their homeland, had known Wojtyla as a bishop and then archbishop of Krakow.

In 1983, Abramowicz traveled with him to Poland. Near every stop, Abramowicz recalled, the communist government of Poland had mobilized tank battalions, ready to move in and crush anything that looked like a threat to government control. Crowds gathered in dangerous numbers.

The pope never blinked.

"He was a man who identified himself with the peasant, with the scholar, with the artist. You name it, he was intimately interested in these people. He became one with them," Abramowicz remembered in 1999.

"His talks were bold, almost revolutionary, and yet he controlled the crowds completely. There was no violence, no uprising. It was more like a strengthening of convictions."

With Poland's President Lech Walesa, Warsaw, 1991

Influence on political situations

In the years since the fall of the Berlin Wall, journalists and scholars have debated just what role the pope played in the demise of Soviet communism. In their 1996 biography, Watergate investigative reporter Carl Bernstein and Italian newspaperman Marco Politi speculated that the pope and President Ronald Reagan had made a secret pact to funnel U.S. aid through the church to aid democratic movements behind the Iron Curtain.

Other biographers and scholars have ridiculed such conspiracy theories. Though the pope provided some material assistance behind the scenes, most have argued that his biggest influence on the political situation was through his uncompromising, theologically based preaching for a society that would put human beings first, giving them the freedom of worship, speech and thought.

Far from diminishing his role, that clear and powerful vision proved more effective than any conspiracy—the ultimate answer to the derisive question Soviet strongman Josef Stalin once asked: "How many divisions does the pope have?"

"I believe he was absolutely central to [the fall of communism] ... central to why it happened in the 1980s, and why it happened non-violently," said George Weigel, a Catholic scholar in Washington who was granted more than two years of regular interviews with the pope in preparation for the 1999 biography "Witness to Hope."

The pope, Weigel said, saw his own role in Poland as "a spark in a tinderbox," lighting the intellectual fire that kept the social-labor movement Solidarity alive through years of vicious suppression.

John Paul II tried to provide that spark wherever he encountered oppressive regimes, from Chile to Haiti, the Philippines to Nigeria. Seldom did he point fingers or explicitly side with political factions; he was careful not to embarrass his hosts or provoke a government backlash that would further harm the people.

But starting from Gospel passages and church teachings, his speeches and homilies would hold up an ideal of governments serving people, not vice versa.

When he made his historic visit to Cuba in 1998, addressing one of the few Catholic peoples who had not yet heard his message in person, he began slowly. On his first day, he talked about individual responsibility; on his second, he talked about sacredness of family.

On his third day, he moved to the concept of just communities and national destiny. By his fourth and final day, when a quarter million chanting people had gathered in Havana's Revolution Square, the pope put it all together in a stirring message of hope for the role a freer, more religious Cuba could play in the world.

"He's enacting a drama that has universal significance," said Michael Novak, a scholar of Catholicism at the American Enterprise Institute. "It's an immense thing when a pope shows up in front of a totalitarian and secular power and speaks for liberty."

There was no new revolution in Havana that day, but as on so many trips, the pope did not depart empty-handed. Within weeks, President Fidel Castro announced that he would release 200 prisoners, mostly political, in response to the pope's plea. Later that year, he announced that Christmas would be officially celebrated in the atheist state for the first time in decades.

Through his trips abroad, covering more than 720,000 miles, the prevailing mood was one of euphoria and adoration.

But not all of his travels were so triumphant. During a trip to Belgium and the Netherlands in the mid-1980s, where local bishops and the Vatican had recently cracked down on popular liberal theologians, cheers for the pope were mixed with boos and heckling.

Elsewhere in Europe, and especially in the United States, some observers worried that the enthusiastic greetings the pope received had more to do with celebrity worship than with any particular devotion to the message he was carrying.

"His visits work two ways," said Richard McBrien, a theologian and papal scholar at the University of Notre Dame. "In places like the U.S., it boosts the morale of the conservative Catholics and the cultural Catholics. But it's also a reminder of the negative aspects of his papacy. For some, John Paul represents a too rigid, too repressive idea of life in the church.

"The real question one has to ask is: What kind of lasting effects do these trips have? Is there any evidence that his visits have a lasting effect on the local churches?"

Teaching, writing have shaped church

If it is difficult to estimate the lasting effects of a pope's personal presence, even a presence as compelling as John Paul II's, there is little doubt that his teaching and writing have shaped the church for generations to come.

His writing is bound to wield influence over a wide swath of issues that face the church. He wrote 14 encyclicals, the highest form of papal discourse, along with 14 apostolic exhortations, 10 apostolic constitutions, 44 apostolic letters, hundreds of other documents and several books.

Print was not his only medium. Just before Easter 1999, a compact disc that mixed recordings of papal addresses with songs and prayers by the pope was released, supported by a music video.

Most writing that comes under the papal seal is the product of collaboration. In the 1999 exhortation "Church in America," for instance, it was a committee of bishops, working from the deliberations of a 200-bishop synod, that cobbled together the first draft.

Chicago Cardinal Francis George, who was part of that drafting committee, said the pope put his stamp on the document by putting it in theological context, by grounding the bishops' practical recommendations in Scripture and church teaching.

With his encyclicals and other major documents, John Paul II was even more directly involved, taking the unusual step of writing his own first drafts.

Like his prayer life, writing was a discipline he practiced rigorously, devoting a couple of hours each morning to working on whatever project was at hand. With his training in philosophy and theology, the results have provided scholars and churchmen with material for lifetimes of study.

In one encyclical, "The Splendor of Truth," the pope made an impassioned argument against the moral and metaphysical relativism that has seeped through modern culture, often coloring the thought of people who are unaware of the philosophy underlying it.

In another encyclical, he put the church's traditional teachings on wealth and work into a modern context in which capitalism has triumphed over competing economic systems, while globalization undermines the most basic assumptions people have about their livelihoods.

Smaller works included a landmark apology to Jews for the church's longstanding institutional bias against them, with a controversial discussion of the role of the Catholic Church during the Holocaust. Another letter emphatically declared that women cannot be priests; and others touched on the nature of Catholic colleges, war and peace, and the future of the church in Africa.

One of his most ambitious pieces was "Faith and Reason," an encyclical released in the fall of 1998, on the eve of his 20th anniversary as pope.

In more than 100 pages of complex but lucid reasoning, the pope made the case for why religion is not only possible but a necessary response to scientific advancement, postmodern doubt about the nature of truth, and all that has transformed human attitudes in the 20th Century.

At times specific and technical, at times as wide-ranging and universal, "Faith and Reason" was widely seen as a fitting capstone to more than half a century of John Paul II's intellectual career.

Though portions of that encyclical, like most everything the pope wrote, said or did over the years, provoked controversy and passion, some have argued that this grand philosophical work is an important cornerstone upon which the church can rebuild itself for the third millennium of Christianity.

Leading the church into millennium

John Paul II thought often about the new millennium.

At the outset of a 1999 trip to Poland, facing a grueling itinerary of 21 cities over 13 days, the pontiff told a crowd of a prophecy given him by his former mentor, Cardinal Stefan Wyszynski.

"If God has chosen you, he has chosen you to lead the church into the next millennium," Wyszynski told then-Cardinal Wojtyla shortly before his election to pope.

John Paul II took that responsibility seriously. He declared 2000 a Jubilee year, a focused period of devotion in which Catholics could earn indulgences by making pilgrimages to the holiest sites of the faith. He ordered three years of theological preparation throughout the church, focusing on the Father, the Son and the Holy Spirit of the Christian Trinity.

He also saw 2000 as a time to look beyond Roman Catholicism. The millennium, as he saw it, was a compelling moment for Christianity to put behind the schisms that had divided it for nearly 1,000 years. He put special emphasis on mending relations with Orthodox Christians, making his first visit to an Orthodox nation, Romania, in 1999.

He also made major overtures to other Christians, Jews and Muslims.

The heart of the Jubilee, and one of the crowning moments of his papacy, was a series of trips retracing the story of Christian faith. While political conflict prevented a proposed trip to a site believed to be the ancient city of Ur, in modern Iraq, the pope traveled in February 2000 to Egypt, to walk in the footsteps of Moses.

Standing atop Mt. Nebo where, tradition says, Moses first saw the Promised Land, Jordan, 2000

In March 2000, he traveled to Jordan, Israel and Palestinian territories, his first visit there as pope and only the second papal visit to the Holy Land. He stared out over the desert from Mt. Nebo, where Moses was said to have sighted the Holy Land, then prayed in a driving sandstorm at an archeological site where John the Baptist may have baptized Jesus.

Then, in Israel, the pope mixed the journey of faith with the issues of the moment. He seemed most joyous celebrating a mass for young people on a hillside overlooking the Sea of Galilee, noting how the fishing boats plying the lake reminded him of the fishermen whom Jesus made disciples.

Two events in Jerusalem cemented his bond with the Jewish people. First, the pope went to Yad Vashem, the Holocaust memorial, where he prayed and met with survivors. Then, on his last day, he went to the Western Wall, the holiest site in Judaism, believed to be the visible remainder of the ancient Temple. There, the pontiff bent his head near the pitted stone and prayed silently before leaving a small written prayer stuffed into a crack in the wall, surrounded by the thousands of notes and prayers Jews leave there every day.

Commentators noted how carefully the pope had steered through the political risks of the trip, acknowledging the suffering of the Palestinians without endorsing their political agenda; strengthening bonds with Israel, while not forgetting the Arab Muslims and Christians who live in the minority there.

For most observers, it was the intensely personal and holy nature of the pope's presence that provided the lasting memories.

Only briefly did that triumphant journey silence the growing hubbub about the pope's health, however. Again and again, rumors of ill health or retirement swirled around the Vatican.

By the Jubilee year, even doctors observing him wondered how long he would be able to keep up the kind of demanding public ministry he and the world expected.

For most of the last decade he was troubled by the symptoms of Parkinson's disease. Eventually he became bent in a permanent hunch, his walk reduced to a shuffle and his hands beset by tremors. The syndrome also slurred his speech and limited the expressions of his once-lively face. Even minor ailments—viruses, coughs, fevers—began to intrude on his activities.

Still, the journey continued. During a six-day trip in May 2001, the pope traced the steps of St. Paul the Apostle in Greece, Syria and Malta. In Damascus, he became the first Roman Catholic pontiff to visit a mosque to highlight his appeal for peace and brotherhood among Christians, Muslims and Jews.

He told a gathering of imams that he was deeply moved by the visit and hoped that Muslims and Christians would be "communities in respectful dialogue, never more as communities in conflict.

"For all the times that Muslims and Christians have offended one another, we need to seek forgiveness from the Almighty and to offer each other forgiveness," the pope said.

The following month the pope made his first visit to Ukraine amid protests by Orthodox Christians who blamed the West for their social and economic ills.

Again, the pope offered an apology, this time "for errors committed in both the distant and recent past."

Even the terrorist attacks of Sept. 11, 2001, did not stop the pope from spreading his message. Protected by heavy security, he left Sept. 22 for a six-day trip to Kazakhstan and Armenia.

And still the milestones continued. In October 2003, amid another flurry of rumors about impending death, he celebrated the 25th anniversary of his pontificate. Even as Vatican officials sought to extol the virtues of the pontificate, the pope shifted attention away from himself by choosing to beatify Mother Teresa the same weekend, pushing a contemporary and kindred spirit on the fast track to sainthood. By March 2004, his pontificate was longer than all except Pius IX's 31 years and St. Peter's estimated 34 years at the helm of the church.

The pope often referred to his approaching death. But almost always he said it with a smile, and with a window held open by his unshakable faith in God.

On one trip, the pope told a group of his fellow Poles that this might be his last trip to his homeland.

But when they began chanting "Sto Lat"—"May you live to be 100!"—John Paul II said maybe it could happen after all.

He quoted something Cardinal Wyszynski had told him decades earlier. But the pontiff could have been paraphrasing himself from 1,000 other occasions, or simply summarizing the precept on which he based every audacious, unpredictable, faith-filled gesture of his historic career.

"Don't set limits on divine providence," he said. And as so many times before, hundreds of thousands of adoring followers broke out into joyous cheers. ■

Steve Kloehn
Chicago Tribune

CLEMENS·X·PONT·MAX·
ANNO·IVBILEI·MDCLXXV·

In a ceremony to seal
the Holy Door of St.
Peter's Basilica, 2001

Chapter 1

Latin America:
The pilgrimage begins

In 1979, not long after being installed as pope, John Paul II made his first papal trip abroad, to Latin America. While praying in Mexico City before an image of the Virgin Mary, he had an epiphany that would shape the long pontificate that lay before him.

He saw that he would become a pilgrim with the whole world as his destination. He would tour the globe much as a parish priest might tour his parish. Like that priest, he would inspire and comfort and teach and admonish. He would do this not just as head of the church speaking remotely from the Vatican, but as the church's living, breathing manifestation, a physical presence at the eye of the storm of attention that surrounded him.

It was one thing to issue a statement chastising some of the Latin American clergy for their political activism, but the message came simpler and stronger when the pope stood in front of a Nicaraguan priest and shook his finger in the man's face. His thoughts on the inhumanity of the exploitation of laborers had real muscle when delivered amid thousands of poor, indigenous people in Cuilapam de Guerrero, Mexico.

"The pope wants to be your voice," he told them, "the voice of those who cannot speak or are silent; the defender of the oppressed, who have the right to effective help, not charity or the crumbs of justice." ◼

Cuilapam
de Guerrero,
Mexico, 1979

Puebla, Mexico, 1979

Top: Rio de Janeiro, 1997
Left: Puebla, Mexico, 1979
Above: Mexico City, 2002
Facing page: Cakchiqueles tribespeople, Guatemala City, 1983

Military base, Guatemala City, 1983

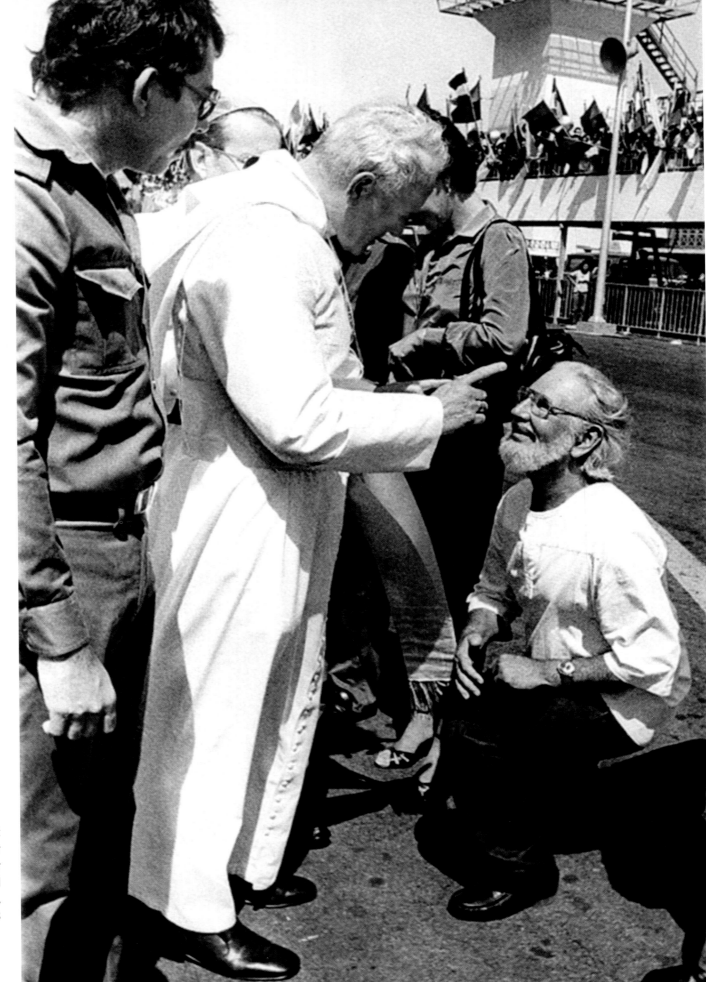

Chiding priest
and Culture Minister
Ernesto Cardenal for
mixing politics and
religion, Managua,
Nicaragua, 1983

Salta, Argentina, 1987

Right: Passing the Che Guevara mural
Below: Mass in Sacred Heart Church, Havana
Facing page: Greeted by President Fidel Castro on the pope's only visit to Cuba, José Martí Airport, Havana, 1998

Watching a native
dancer during a mass
at the Basilica of the
Virgin of Guadalupe,
Mexico City, 2002

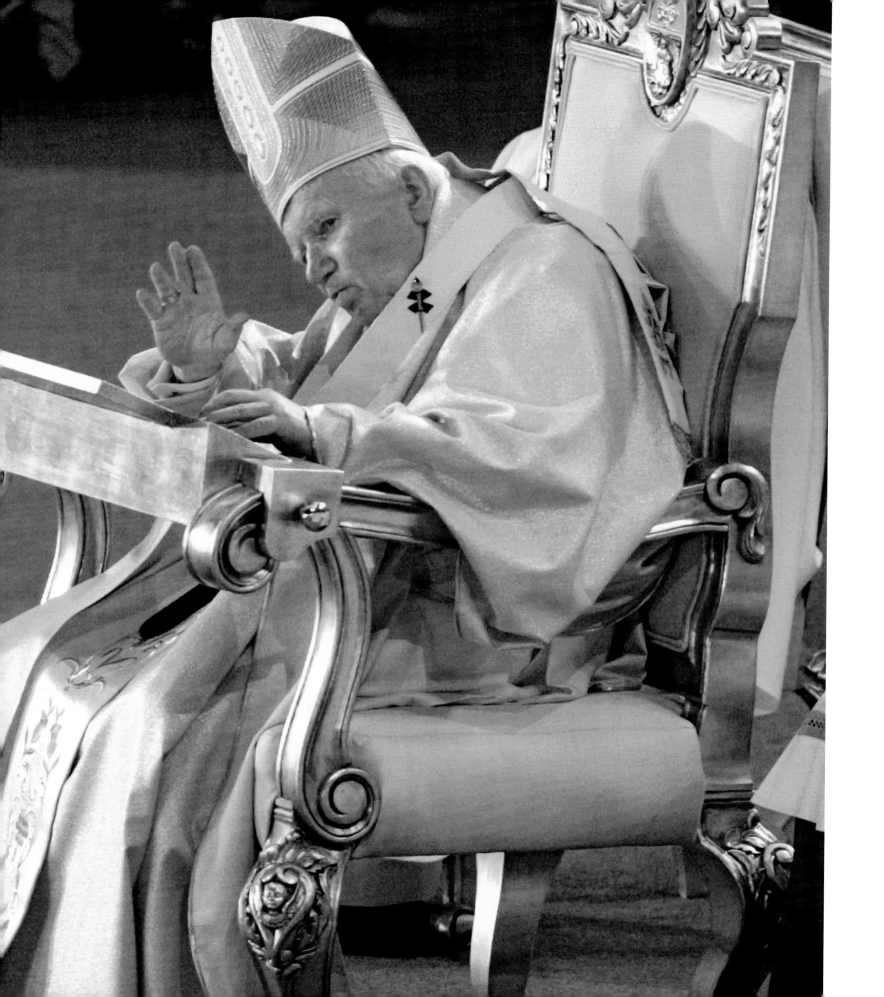

Chapter 2

Poland: Breaking the grip of communism

Born in southern Poland near Krakow, Karol Wojtyla grew to be a priest, of course, but he also was an actor, hiker, playwright, kayaker, philosopher and—during Nazi occupation and, later, communist rule—a witness to evil.

Wojtyla had friends in Krakow's Jewish community, which was nearly obliterated when Nazis murdered many of its people outright and sent others to the death camp at nearby Auschwitz. For this pope, revulsion toward anti-Semitism was personal.

He was the first pope to have lived under communism, a system he felt robbed people of their humanity. When he was elected, the Poles felt a tremendous psychological lift. The pope, however, would prove to be more than just a symbolic ally.

On his first visit home as pope in 1979, he laid the intellectual foundation for the labor movement Solidarity. On his second visit in 1983, John Paul II confronted his reluctant host, Gen. Wojciech Jaruzelski, Poland's leader. With the pope's support, the Polish people forced one of the first cracks in Soviet communism.

Jaruzelski seemed shaky when he greeted the pope. He said he was nervous because his prepared speech had not yet arrived. Others in his regime later said it was because he realized the pope's message of human dignity carried inexorable power. He saw the pontiff's visit as the beginning of the end. ■

First visit to his homeland since becoming pope, Warsaw military airport, 1979

Warsaw's Victory Square
cleared for helicopter
arrival, 1979

Above: Solidarity demonstration after a service held by the pope in his home city of Krakow, 1983
Facing page: Solidarity leader Lech Walesa (left) with church-appointed mediator Tadeusz Mazowiecki
as they leave the Lenin Shipyard having ended an eight-day strike in Gdansk, 1988

Above: Security forces restraining the crowd that awaits the pope, Czestochowa, 1983
Right: Under martial law imposed to prevent Solidarity from gaining power, Warsaw, 1982

Meeting with an uneasy Polish Gen. Wojciech Jaruzelski, Krakow, 1983

Assisted in ascending the
stairs to the podium,
Lubaczow, 1991

Greeted before papal mass, Krakow, 2002

Overlooking the mountains
near Zakopane in southern
Poland, 1997

Above: Visiting his parents' and older brother's graves at Rakowicki
cemetery, Krakow, 2002
Facing page: Surprise visit to members of the Milewski family,
farmers in the village of Leszczewo in northeast Poland, 1999

Krakow, 2002

Chapter 3

North America: Stranger in a strange land

In 1979, on his first papal visit to North America, John Paul II stood before 75,000 people in Yankee Stadium in New York City, the city where, if you "can make it there, you can make it anywhere." There, of all places, he decried the excesses of materialism.

He said Christians must make "a decisive break with the frenzy of consumerism, exhausting and joyless. It is not a question of slowing down progress, for there is no human progress when everything conspires to give full rein to self interest, sex and power."

By emphasizing the traditional values of Catholicism, including stands against divorce and the sexual revolution, he was challenging what seemed to him the rapid erosion of morality throughout the modern world. Nowhere was that erosion seen more clearly than in the U.S.

Despite his countercultural stance, he was greeted like a celebrity. Time magazine called him "John Paul, Superstar." When he came to Madison Square Garden to tell tens of thousands of teenagers to accept moral responsibility for their lives, a school band played the theme from the popular movie "Rocky."

Some Americans might have ignored his message or been made uncomfortable by it, but most found this pope personally irresistible. At that gathering of teens, when the crowd chanted, "John Paul II, we love you," he answered, "John Paul II, he loves you." ■

Chicago, 1979

Grant Park, Chicago, 1979

Chicago, 1979

Above: Souvenirs, San Antonio, 1987
Right: Traditional Polish dress at Five Holy Martyrs Church, Chicago, 1979
Facing page, top: Los Angeles, 1987
Facing page, bottom: Chicago's Southwest Side, 1979

69

Papal mass, Boston, 1979

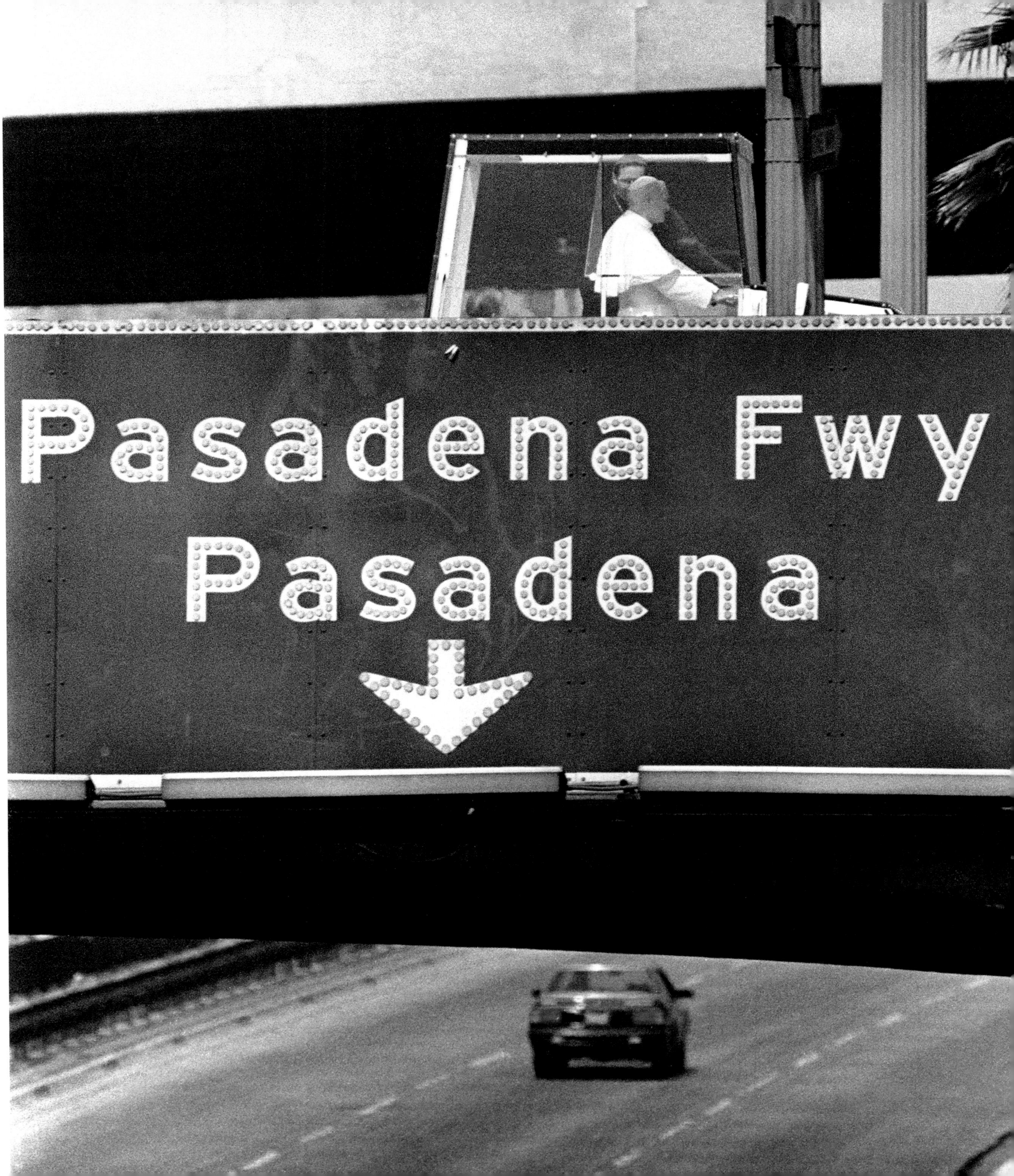
Pasadena Fwy
Pasadena

Above: Embracing a 5-year-old AIDS patient, San Francisco, 1987
Facing page: Popemobile on overpass, Los Angeles, 1987

Above: Preaching abstinence from drugs and sex to young people
in New Orleans' Superdome, 1987
Facing page: Pima tribe purification ceremony, Phoenix, 1987

A conversation with
President Ronald Reagan
in the glare of TV lights,
Miami, 1987

Saying the rosary while
walking through the
woods, Elk Island National
Park, Alberta, 1984

Above: Toronto, 1984
Right: St. Anne de Beaupre, Quebec, 1984

Above: Windy day in the LeBreton Flats area of Ottawa, 1984
Facing page: World Youth Day, Downsview Park, Toronto, 2002

Twilight, Quebec City, 1984

Chapter 4

The Middle East: Patching old wounds

In a centuries-old ritual, Jews insert messages written on small pieces of paper into cracks in Jerusalem's Western Wall. During his millennium-year visit to the Holy Land, John Paul II joined in this tradition to give a historic message to the Jewish people.

Without specifically fixing blame, his note asked forgiveness for the suffering Jews had endured over the years. In it, he pledged to "commit ourselves to genuine brotherhood with the people of the covenant." It was a landmark moment in a career of outreach.

He was the first pope ever to set foot in the main synagogue in Rome, home to the city's 2,000-year-old Jewish community. He was the first pope to enter a mosque. He met with Sunni Muslim clerics in Cairo. At the foot of Mt. Sinai, he entered a 6th Century Greek Orthodox monastery, a step toward mending an estrangement 1,000 or more years old.

He said that Roman Catholicism had developed the rational aspect of the faith while Orthodoxy had embraced the mystic, and that each needed the other. His had been an influential voice in the Second Vatican Council, which called for Eastern and Western faiths to join so that the church could "breathe with two lungs."

The pope was able to encompass seeming contradictions. While playing up the similarities of various faiths, he also underscored the uniqueness of Catholicism by emphasizing the Virgin Mary and insisting that clergy wear priestly garb to set them apart from the secular world. ■

God of our fathers,
you chose Abraham and his descendants
to bring your Name to the Nations:
we are deeply saddened
by the behaviour of those
who in the course of history
have caused these children of yours to suffer,
and asking your forgiveness
we wish to commit ourselves
to genuine brotherhood
with the people of the Covenant.

Jerusalem, 26 March 2000

Joannes Paulus II

Pilgrims waving Palestinian, Vatican, Israeli and Lebanese flags before a papal mass by the Sea of Galilee, Israel, 2000

Above: At the residence of Sunni Muslim leader Sheik Mohammed Sayed Tantawi (third from left), Cairo, 2000

Facing page: St. Catherine's Greek Orthodox Monastery, where Moses is said to have received the 10 Commandments, Mt. Sinai, Egypt, 2000

Above: Palestinian child waving his country's flag, Deheisha refugee camp near Bethlehem, 2000
Facing page: Local Christians at a papal mass by the Sea of Galilee, Israel, 2000

At Jerusalem's Western Wall, Judaism's holiest site, 2000

Chapter 5

The globe: Touching humanity one soul at a time

For years, each time John Paul II reached his destination and got off the plane, he knelt and kissed the ground, emphasizing that every place on Earth is sacred, that the planet we all share is holy ground. Later, as age and illness made him unsteady, a small container of soil would be brought to him and lifted to his lips.

Often, when he faced millions, news reports would talk of "speaking to the masses." He never thought of it that way. To him, those seas of upturned faces were millions of unique souls, each posing a question for which the answer is Christ.

He spoke the languages of most who came to him. In addition to the Latin used in the mass, the pope was fluent in Polish, English, Italian, Spanish, German, Lithuanian and French and, when necessary, learned phrases of languages outside his grasp.

Not that everyone who understood his words agreed with them. His unyielding stands on controversial issues sometimes made him the target of protest. On a visit to Germany, for instance, his popemobile was spattered with red paint.

In an era of mass communication, he understood globally what a candidate for councilman understands locally: the power of personal appearance. Anyone who ever stood on tiptoes in a throng of people just to get a glimpse of him tells later of when "I saw the pope." ■

In flight during a tour
of the U.S., 1987

Above: Bosnian Croat waiting for papal mass at Kosevo Stadium, Sarajevo, 1997
Left: A South Korean congregation, 1984
Facing page: Baku airport, Azerbaijan, 2002

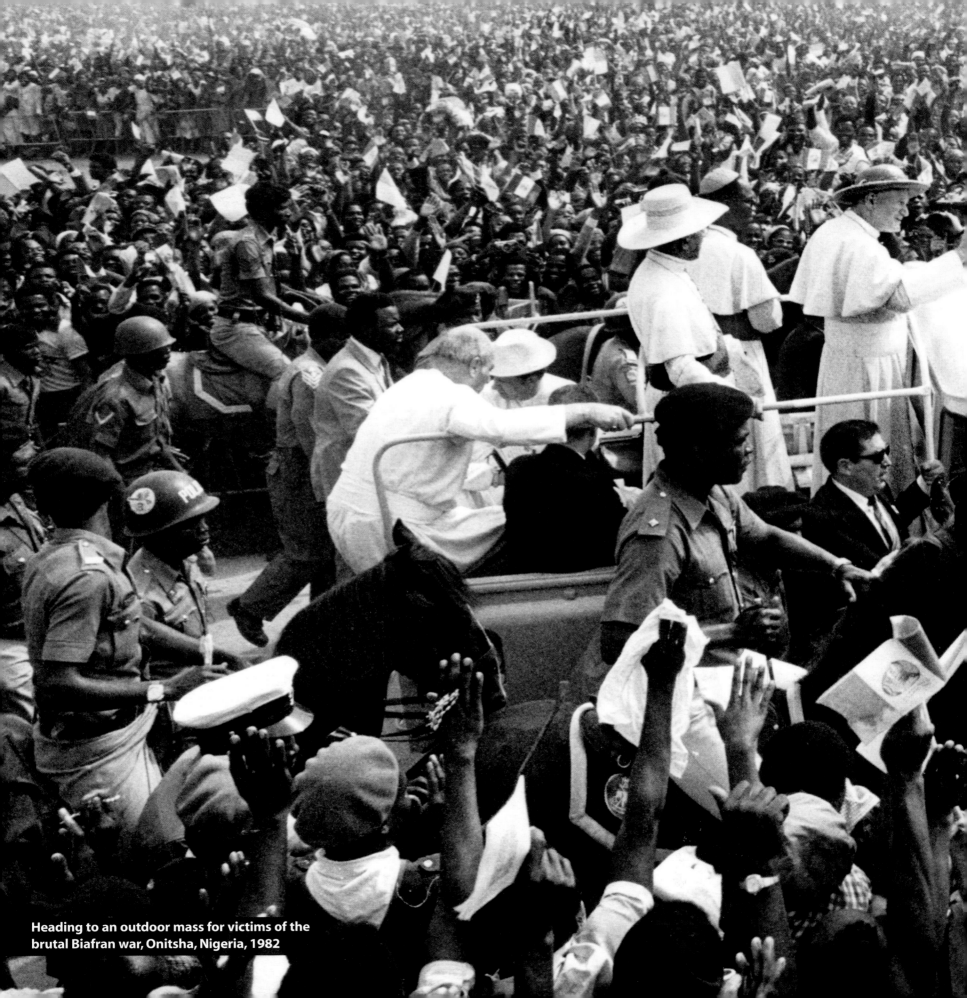

Heading to an outdoor mass for victims of the brutal Biafran war, Onitsha, Nigeria, 1982

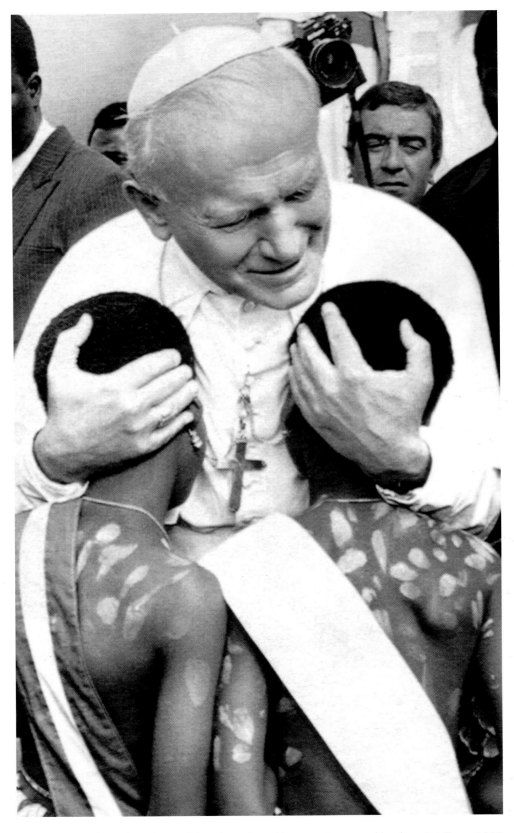

Above: Boys in traditional northern Togo costume and body paint, Togo, 1985
Right: Blessing a child with leprosy at a hospital in Cumura, Guinea-Bissau, World Leper Day, 1990

Mother Teresa,
Calcutta, India, 1986

Above: Nuns of the Hermanas de la Cruz (Sisters of the Cross) order after a papal service in which one of their members was canonized, Plaza Colon, Madrid, 2003
Right: King Juan Carlos and Queen Sofia of Spain after receiving a papal blessing in Madrid's central square

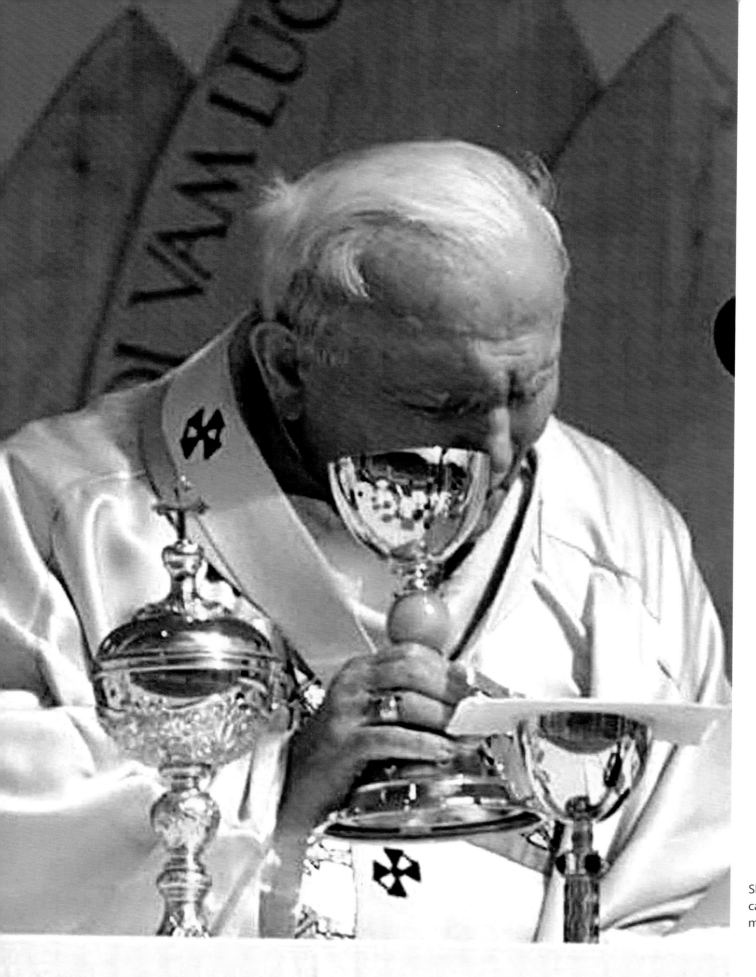

Skullcap, called a *zuchetto*, carried off by wind as he offers mass in Maribor, Slovenia, 1999

The grotto where, in 1858, the Virgin Mary is said to have appeared to Bernadette Soubirou, Lourdes, France, 2004

Chapter 1

The pontiff

When the head of the world's largest church was not on the road, John Paul II, the 264th bishop of Rome, was surrounded by the marble floors, the Renaissance paintings, the Swiss Guards, the baroque grandeur of the Vatican, his command center, his office, his home.

Early on, he made it clear to his staff that he would set the tone for his pontificate. He told security people to step aside so he could wade into crowds to touch and be touched. He insisted on referring to himself as "I" or "me" rather than the royal "we" most popes had used.

He did most of his writing in the Vatican. He was a prolific producer of encyclicals, apostolic exhortations, constitutions, letters and other documents, often writing for hours in longhand. Beyond his church writings, he produced several popular books and participated in CDs containing songs, prayers and speeches.

He also was prolific in proclaiming saints, canonizing and beatifying far more than all previous popes together. It was part of his global view, an effort to show that saints are not just part of a long-ago Europe, but could appear any-where on Earth, especially in response to the challenges of the modern world.

The first non-Italian pope in more than four centuries made the Vatican his as he, sometimes controversially, sometimes historically, shaped the church. He visited the world as the pilgrim pope. In Rome, the world came to him. ■

Flanked by Cardinal Edmund Casimir Szoka (left) and Bishop Piero Marini (right) after a ceremony to inaugurate the restored Sistine Chapel, 1999

Pilgrims gathered in St. Peter's Square after the beatification of Popes Pius IX and John XXIII, 2000

Surrounded by members of the Congregation for the Doctrine of the Faith in Clementine Hall at the Vatican, 2004

Above: Entering the pontiff's studio in the Vatican with South African President Nelson Mandela, 1998
Facing page: American singer-songwriter Bob Dylan performing "Knocking on Heaven's Door," Bologna, 1997

Above: Sending a message to bishops on a computer bearing the papal seal, the first such use of the Internet for a pope, 2001
Right: Signing the Ecclesia de Eucharistia encyclical, 2003
Facing page: In the pope's private Vatican library, American cardinals, including Boston's Cardinal Bernard Law (far left) attending a closed-door session on the clergy sex-abuse scandal, 2002

Before a bronze and brass sculpture of the Resurrection by Pericle Fazzini, the pope's regular Wednesday general audience in the Vatican's Paul VI Hall, 2003

Pilgrims from Chicago gathering for a photo with the pope, 2003

Above: Blessing a child in Castel Gandolfo near Rome, 2004
Facing page: Acknowledging the crowd after the beatification ceremony for Padre Pio, a mystic Italian monk, whose image hangs on the St. John Basilica in Lateran Square, 1999

Surrounded by Pentecostal
bishops from the U.S., 2004

Above: Lights in the top floor windows from the papal apartments overlooking St. Peter's Square, 2003
Facing page: In his private chapel, praying for the victims of the terrorist bomb attack in Madrid, 2004

Chapter 2

The victim

It was common to see hands rising from the crowds as John Paul II passed, hands waving, hands holding cameras, hands reaching out to him. But one spring day in May 1981, as his jeep passed through St. Peter's Square, one hand rising above the throng held a pistol.

Two shots were fired. One bullet grazed him, but the other hit a hand and ricocheted, tearing through his abdomen, "miraculously" (one of the doctors said) missing his vital organs.

Shortly after regaining consciousness, the pope forgave his assailant, Mehmet Ali Agca, an escaped Turkish murderer. After recuperation, John Paul II appeared in the square where he had been shot and thanked God for permitting him "to experience suffering, and the danger of losing my life."

Later he visited Agca in prison. Their conversation was never revealed, but, at one point, Agca bent to kiss the pope's hand. Sitting with the man who had tried to kill him gave flesh and blood and breath to the virtue of forgiveness the pope long had espoused.

Just nine months after the attack, he was back in the air, heading for Africa, more determined than ever to pursue his pilgrimage. ▪

Gunman in the crowd to the left
moments before shots were fired

Wounded, slumping in his vehicle

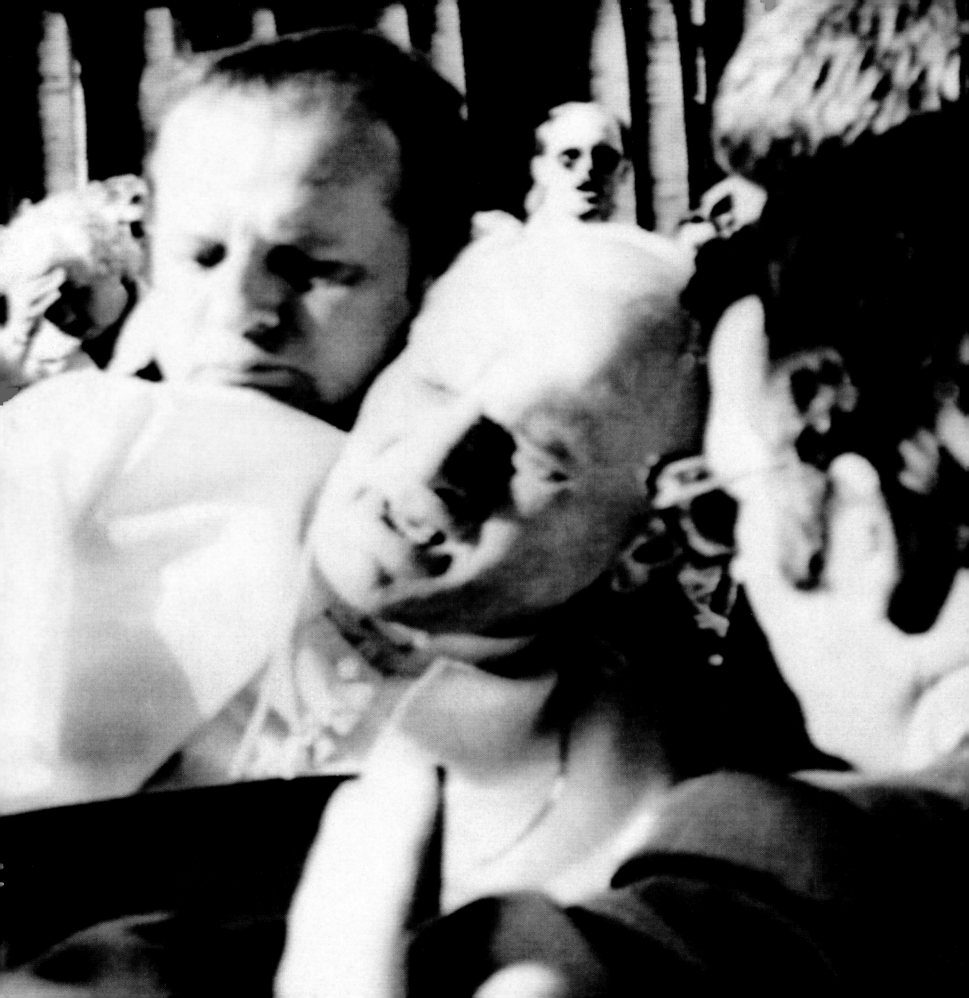

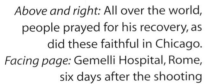

Above and right: All over the world, people prayed for his recovery, as did these faithful in Chicago. *Facing page:* Gemelli Hospital, Rome, six days after the shooting

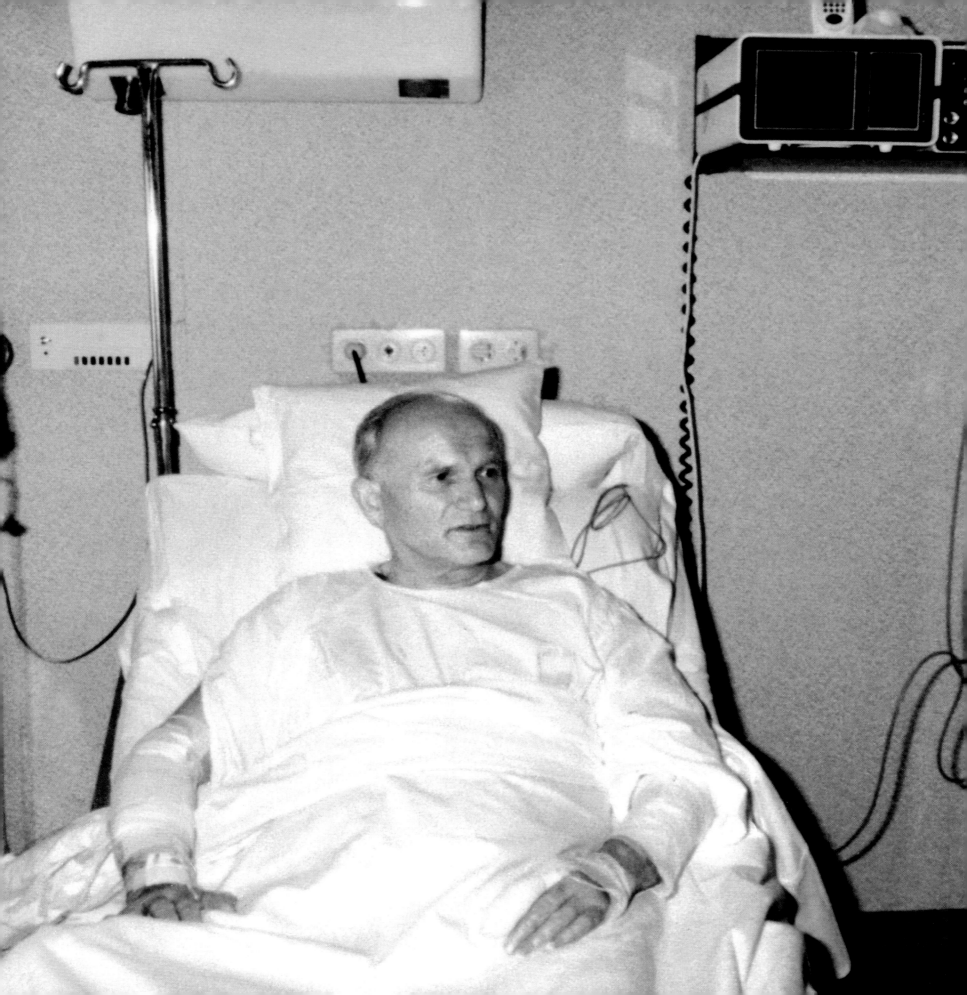

Above: Agca, 1985
Facing page: Showing forgiveness
for his assailant, Mehmet Ali Agca,
in Rebibbia Prison, Rome, 1983

Chapter 3

The priest

Each year, during the week leading up to Easter, the pinnacle of the Christian calendar, John Paul II led services commemorating the death and resurrection of Christ. The week builds to the Triduum (Latin for "three days") that begins with the consecration of the Eucharist on the evening of Holy Thursday. It continues with the Stations of the Cross at the Roman Colosseum on Good Friday, the midnight Easter vigil, and culminates with evening prayers on Easter Sunday.

During the 2003 Easter service, John Paul called for an end "to the chain of hatred and terrorism, which threatens the orderly development of the human family. May God grant that we be free from the peril of a tragic clash between cultures and religions. May faith and love of God make the followers of every religion courageous builders of understanding and forgiveness, patient weavers of a fruitful interreligious dialogue, capable of inaugurating a new era of justice and peace." ■

The dome of St. Peter's at dusk, Holy Week, 2003

Holy Thursday service in
St. Peter's Basilica

The Stations of the Cross at the Colosseum, Good Friday

Above: Consecration of the host, Holy Saturday
Right: Mass, Easter Sunday

Above: Crowding St. Peter's Square,
Easter Sunday, 2003
Right: The Swiss Guards
Facing page: The faithful
undeterred by on-and-off rain

Leaving St. Peter's Square
after Easter mass

Holy Thursday

Chapter 4

The teacher

As a global pilgrim, Pope John Paul II's mission was to travel the world, bringing the word of God to millions. From that inaugural mass in 1979, when "Be not afraid" became his refrain, the homilies he delivered were powerful, his message unflinching.

His words may have carried the lessons, but it was his actions over a 26-year papacy that provided the most vivid example of Christianity.

Early on, he was a living example of forgiveness when he reached out to the man whose bullet nearly killed him. In later years, as his health declined, his perseverance through pain touched the world as he, frail and bent, continued his pilgrimage–sometimes struggling, but never retreating.

And in his final act, John Paul II's public lesson about dignity and dying was a poignant message on the value of life. He faced the world until the end, using the opportunity, as he wrote in a message to priests, to unite "my own sufferings with those of Christ." ▪

Mourner in
St. Peter's Square

Pope John Paul II
1920-2005

Chicago Tribune

Publisher
David Hiller

Editor
Ann Marie Lipinski

Managing editor
James O'Shea

John Paul II
THE EPIC LIFE OF A PILGRIM POPE

Photo editor
José Moré

Editors
Steve Kloehn
Charles Leroux
Jill Boba

Imagers
Don Bierman
Christine Bruno
Kathy Celer

Project managers
Tony Majeri Jr.
Bill Parker
Susan Zukrow

Designer
Eileen Wagner,
Wagner/Donovan Design

Photo credits

COVER
Amy Sancetta/AP: front cover
Archive of "The Family Home of John Paul II"
Karol Wojtyla, age 18: back cover
Anne Cusack/Chicago Tribune: back cover

INTRODUCTION
Amy Sancetta/AP: title page
AP: 4-5
Paolo Cocco/Reuters: 6-7
Jean-Marc Bouju/AP: 8-9
José Moré/Chicago Tribune: 10-11
Jean-Claude Delmas/AFP/Getty: 12-13
Gabriel Bouys/AFP/Getty: 14-15

BOOK 1
AP: 16, 21, 23
Archive of "The Family Home of John Paul II": 19
Catholic News Service: 20
Chicago Tribune files: 22
José Moré/Chicago Tribune: 24
Rainer Klostermeier/AP: 26
Arturo Mari/Reuters: 29
Arturo Mari/AP: 31

BOOK 2
CHAPTER 1: LATIN AMERICA
José Moré/UPI: 33
Anne Cusack/Chicago Tribune: 34-35,
37 (bottom left)
Pete Leabo/AP: 36, 38-39, 41
Arturo Mari/AP: 37 (top)
Susana Gonzalez/Getty: 37 (bottom right)
AP: 40
José Moré /Chicago Tribune: 42-43
Heriberto Rodriguez/Reuters: 44-45

CHAPTER 2: POLAND
UPI: 47, 52 (top)
Hugo Peralta/UPI: 48-50
Cezary Sokolowski/AP: 51
AP: 52 (bottom), 54, 56-57
AP/Interpress: 53 (bottom)
Jerry Lampen/Reuters: 55
Vatican: 58
Pier Paolo Cito/AP: 59
Vincenzo Pinto/AP: 60-61

CHAPTER 3: NORTH AMERICA
Charles Osgood/Chicago Tribune: 63
Ed Wagner Jr./Chicago Tribune: 64-65
Ovie Carter/Chicago Tribune: 66
Bob Fila/Chicago Tribune: 67, 70-71
Chris Walker/Chicago Tribune: 68 (top), 69 (top), 72,
Frank Hanes/Chicago Tribune: 68 (bottom)
Ernie Cox Jr./Chicago Tribune: 69 (bottom)
José Moré/Chicago Tribune: 73-75, 80-82, 84-85
Pete Souza/White House: 76-77
Vatican: 78-79
Kevin Frayer/AP: 83

CHAPTER 4: THE MIDDLE EAST
Jim Hollander/Reuters: 87
Francois Guillot/AFP/Getty: 88-89
Arturo Mari/AP: 90
Amr Nabil/AP: 91
Roni Schutzer/Newsmakers: 92
Vincenzo Pinto/Reuters: 93
Gabriel Bouys/Reuters: 94-95

CHAPTER 5: THE GLOBE
Daniel Goodrich/Newsday: 97
Shamil Zhumatov/Reuters: 98
Charles Osgood/Chicago Tribune: 99 (top)
Dennis Brack/Black Star: 99 (bottom)
APN: 100-101
Giulio Broglio/AP: 102
Lusa-Moura/AFP: 103
AP: 104-105
Denis Doyle/AP: 106
Pierre-Philippe Marcou/AFP/Getty: 107
Massimo Sambucetti/AP: 108-109
Splash News: 110-111

BOOK 3
CHAPTER 1: THE PONTIFF
Paolo Cocco/Reuters: 113
Arturo Mari/AP: 114-115, 121
AP: 116-118
Luca Bruno/AP: 119
Massimo Sambucetti/AP: 120 (top)
José Moré/Chicago Tribune: 120 (bottom),
122-125, 131
Filippo Monteforte/EPA: 126
Plinio Lepri/AP:127-129
Reuters: 130

CHAPTER 2: THE VICTIM
AP: 133-135
Tommy Anderson/AP: 136-137
Chicago Tribune files: 138
Arturo Mari/AP: 139-140
Giulio Broglio/AP: 141

CHAPTER 3: THE PRIEST
José Moré/Chicago Tribune: 143-155

CHAPTER 4: THE TEACHER
José Moré/Chicago Tribune: 157-159